MUNDO MAYA

THOR JANSON
BELIZE • EL SALVADOR • GUATEMALA • HONDURAS • MEXICO
Ecology • Indigenous People • Archeology • Festivals • Wildlife

Mundo Maya

Golfo de México

RESERVA NATURAL
RIO LAGARTOS

● CANCUN

● MERIDA

CHICHEN ITZA

ISLA DE
COZUMEL

UXMAL

PENINSULA DE
YUCATAN

TULUM

● CAMPECHE

BIOSFERA DE
SIAN KA'AN

DESCRIPCION

Parques Nacionales, Biosferas
y Reservas Naturales
National Parks, Biosphers and
Natural Reserves

Límites Internacionales
International Borders

Sitios Arqueológicos
Archaeological Sites

● Ciudades Principales
Principal Cities

BIOSFERA
CALK MUL

CHETUMAL ●

LA VENTA

VILLA HERMOSA ●

RIO USUMACINTA

CALAKMUL

ALTÚN HA

EL MIRADOR

BELIZE ● BELIZE CITY

BIOSFERA MAYA

MEXICO

SAN CRISTOBAL
DE LAS CASAS

TIKAL

XUNANTUNICH

Mar Caribe

TÚXTLA
GUTIERREZ ●

YAXCHILAN

● FLORES

CARACOL

● DANGRIGA

BIOSFERA
MONTES AZULES

● POPTUN

MONTAÑAS MAYAS

SIERRA MADRE

● PUNTAGORDA

ISLAS DE LA BAHIA

LA CEIBA

GUATEMALA

SIERRA DE LOS CUCHUMATANES

PARQUE NACIONAL
PICO BONITO

BIOSFERA
RIO PLATANO

PUERTO
LEMPIRA ●

SAN PEDRO SULA ●

QUIRIGUA

QUETZALTENANGO ●

CIUDAD DE
GUATEMALA ●

COPAN

PARQUE NACIONAL
AZUL MEAMBAR

HONDURAS

KAMINAL
JUYU

EL SALVADOR

TEGUCIGALPA ●

Oceano Pacífico

PUERTO
QUETZAL ●

TAZUMAL

● SAN SALVADOR

NICARAGUA

LA LIBERTAD ●

● LA UNION

Table of Contents

Mundo Maya

El Mundo Maya...the words evoke images of a mysterious lost civilization, of sweltering tropical jungles and unexplored mountain cloud-forests. This is the home of the elusive resplendent quetzal, where jaguars prowl and manatee splash in hidden lagoons. Here also live the descendants of the ancient Maya. Numbering more than five million souls and speaking some thirty languages, the contemporary Mayan people inhabit a territory which extends from southern Mexico through Belize, Guatemala, Honduras, and El Salvador. As we tour through the highlands of Chiapas and Guatemala it soon becomes obvious that we have left "Latin America" far behind and entered into a new and exotic world. Here life continues much as it was a thousand years ago. The silence of dawn is broken by the pat, pat, pat of women making corn tortillas. The family gathers around the hearth—the focal point of their little thatched-roof cottage—for a simple breakfast before the men go out to the fields. The women stay close to home; tending children, creating elegant weavings at their back-strap looms, and preparing nutritious meals from the "three sisters": corn, beans, and squash. Mayan village life is conducted as a ritual. Textile production and corn farming are intimately intertwined with sacred practice. This is a magic world of mystery and delight where visiting travelers are welcomed with genuine hospitality and friendliness. It is the purpose of this book to explore the Mayan world through photographic images accompanied by concise descriptions. We will also take a look at the lives of the regions more recent colonists representing European, African and Asian traditions. We hope you enjoy the trip.

Lake Atitlán National Park, Guatemala
[OPPOSITE]

The World of Green Mystery

High up in the cloud-enshrouded mountain forests of Mayaland the cold mist and exuberant vegetation muffle all sounds. Water is everywhere; dripping through the foliage, flowing in little rivulets, crashing down in majestic falls. Every imaginable shade and pattern of green surrounds us in the soft subdued light. The forest is brimming with life and full of animals, but where are they? They are all around us but they are shy and don't reveal themselves easily. We may pass hours wandering through the cathedral-like forest wondering where the avian residents have gone. Then, something causes us to look up, and there before us quietly sits the sublime presence of a resplendent quetzal. He seems to be observing us but when he notices that we have detected him he is gone, like a bolt of lightning, disappearing into the dense green. The tropical forest does not reveal her secrets quickly. But she does want to be known...and loved. The patient and peaceful visitor will be rewarded again and again with unexpected marvels and beauty of glorious intensity. The clouds may engulf our mountain for many days when suddenly one evening, as we warm ourselves by the campfire, the entire sky opens up unveiling the deep black of space and its diamond encrusted eternity.

Down below, in the hot lowland jungle, a very different world awaits us. This is the realm of the jaguar. It's noisier here. The loud grik, grik, grik of a toucan vies with the screeching cacophony of a flock of parrots. The heat sometimes goes beyond what is comfortable and a dip in the crystal clear stream is inviting. Surprisingly, the water is deliciously cold, having just plunged down from the towering peaks above. Although we don't see any, we can be pretty sure that there are crocodile watching us. You rarely spot them in the daytime, but take a strong flashlight and shine it along the river edge at night and the red glowing eyes of an enormous reptile will often be seen. Fortunately, it is extremely rare that they ever bother humans. Nevertheless...

The extreme variety and diversity of life found in the tropical forests of Central America is due to the fact that for millions of years this area has been the biological crossroads of the continent. Climate changes brought on by glacial and inter-glacial periods caused many species to be funneled into the narrow isthmus causing a mixing and blending of forms which has yielded today's unique diversity. Mountain lions, coyotes and raccoons share habitat with kinkajous, tapirs, and howler monkeys. Maples and oaks grow alongside mahoganies and zapotes. And although scientists have uncovered much concerning the workings of these tropical ecosystems, the incredible complexity of interactions of all these thousands of organisms working in concert to make up the living whole simply boggles the mind. Welcome to the land of green mystery.

Resplendent Quetzal *Pharomacrus mocinno*
[OPPOSITE]
SIERRA YALIHÚX, ALTA VERAPAZ PROVINCE, GUATEMALA • The male quetzal's spectacular emerald green and ruby red colors and meter-long serpentine tail so inspired the Maya and Aztecs that they named their central god-man deities after him: Kukulcan and Quetzalcoatl.

Spider Monkey *Ateles geoffroyi*
[OPPOSITE, LEFT]

IXOBEL NATURE RESERVE, GUATEMALA • Extremely agile, these medium sized monkeys can be seen leaping through the canopy from limb to limb in exuberant feats of acrobatics. Their fully prehensile tail serves as a fifth hand and they are often seen hanging upside down, sustained only by their tail and hind paw, tranquilly munching a savory fruit or nut.

Paca *Agouti paca*
[OPPOSITE, TOP RIGHT]

MAYA BIOSPHERE RESERVE, GUATEMALA • Called *Tepescuinle* in Spanish and *Gibnut* in Belize, these large rodents roam the forest floor in search of succulent shoots and nuts. When the Queen of England made her royal visit to Belize some years ago she was served up a plate of gibnut at the dinner ceremony. Visiting dignitaries commented that "she seemed to enjoy it."

Tapir *Tapirus bairdii*
[OPPOSITE, BOTTOM RIGHT]

CALAKMUL BIOSPHERE RESERVE, CAMPECHE, MEXICO • The Tapir, known locally as the "danta" or mountain cow in the case of Belize, is the largest native terrestrial herbivore in the Americas. Adults reach a length of nearly six feet and weigh seven hundred pounds. Over the millenia tapirs have established well defined paths during foraging missions.

Margay *Felis weidii*
[TOP RIGHT]

CALAKMUL BIOSPHERE RESERVE, CAMPECHE, MEXICO • Monkeylike climbing ability distinguishes this rare cat as the most arboreal of the Mesoamerican felines. Spending much of its time in the rain forest canopy, the margay stalks small mammals and birds, leaping from limb to limb and hanging from branches for extended periods with the help of its semiprehensile tail.

Jaguar *Felis onca*
[BOTTOM RIGHT]

CHIAPAS, MEXICO • The largest and most spectacular cat in the Americas, the jaguar is one of the most commonly seen animal figures in the pre-Columbian art of Mesoamerica.

Kinkajou *Potos flavos*
[TOP]
LAKE ATITLÁN NATIONAL PARK, GUATMALA • These medium-sized monkeylike omnivores live in the forest canopy. Extremely agile and largely nocturnal, kinkajous love sweet foods and are known locally as *ositos mieleros*, "little honey bears".

Jaguarundi *Felis yaguarundi*
[BOTTOM]
RIO BRAVO CONSERVATION AREA, ORANGE WALK DISTRICT, BELIZE • Known locally by the Mayan name "Ekmuch," the jaguarundi has also been called the "otter cat" because of its unusual appearance, red-brown coloration and affinity for water. Jaguarundi are excellent swimmers and rarely climb trees as they search for small mammals, birds and reptiles.

Capuchin Monkey *Cebus capucinus*
[OPPOSITE]
RIO PLATANO BIOSPHERE RESERVE, HONDURAS • Also known as white-faced monkeys, the capuchins are highly social canopy dwellers often seen foraging in bands of ten or fifteen individuals. Sometimes, being intensely curious beasts, they come right down to the edge of a jungle camp to get a better look at their strange two-legged cousins.

Palo de Fuego or Fire Tree
[LEFT]
COPÁN VALLEY, HONDURAS

Yellow Tabibuia Tree
[TOP]
ZACAPA PROVINCE, GUATEMALA

Jacaranda Tree in flower
[CENTER]
LAKE ATITLÁN NATIONAL PARK,
GUATEMALA

Wildflower
[BOTTOM]
MAYA MOUNTAINS, BELIZE

Pink Flamingos
Phoenicopterus ruber
[OPPOSITE]
CELESTÚN NATURE RESERVE,
YUCATÁN, MEXICO • As many as
20,000 flamingoes have been
seen congregating during the
winter months at the Celestún
reserve. They are filter-feeders
and sift mud with their specially
adapted beaks for worms and
small crustations which they find
to be delectable.

Ornate Hawk-Eagle
Spizaetus ornatus
[TOP LEFT]
TIKAL NATIONAL PARK, GUATEMALA • This large, striking bird is distinguished by its black crest and bright cinnamon face and neck. It is still relatively common in the virgin lowland rain forests of Central America. Its prey consists of small mammals, reptiles, birds, and insects.

Resplendent Quetzal feathers
[TOP RIGHT]
Detail.

Scarlet Macaw feathers
[BOTTOM RIGHT]
Detail.

White-fronted Parrot
Amazona albifrons
[BOTTOM LEFT]
DEININGER NATIONAL PARK, EL SALVADOR • These mostly green parrots are very hard to see as they forage in the forest canopy. From time to time they reveal themselves by their loud screeching or may suddenly fly out from the trees like a bunch of shrieking banshees.

Keel-Billed Toucan
Ramphastos sulfuratus
[OPPOSITE]
PICO BONITO NATIONAL PARK, HONDURAS • The largest of three species of toucans found in northern Central America, this beautiful bird is easily identified by its bright yellow breast and huge multicolored bill. Found in the lowland jungle up to an elevation of 2,000 feet.

Linneated Woodpecker
Dryocopus lineatus
[LEFT]
XCACEL NATURE RESERVE, QUINTANA ROO, MEXICO • Woodpeckers hammer into the bark of trees to extract insects and larvae. This beautiful male is seen at the entrance of its nest which was made in a dead coconut palm.

Harpy Eagle *Hapia harpyja*
[TOP]
MAYA BIOSPHERE RESERVE, GUATEMALA • The largest eagle on earth. Howler monkeys are its favorite prey.

Yellow-throated Tiger Heron
Tigrisoma mexicanum
[BOTTOM]
BARRA DE SANTIAGO NATURE RESERVE, EL SALVADOR • This beautiful fishing bird is usually seen hunting around large bodies of water. Common in the lowlands but sometimes seen in highland lakes.

Great Snowy Egret
Camerodius albus
[OPPOSITE]
CROOKED TREE WILDLIFE SANCTUARY, BELIZE • These are fishing birds which frequent low elevation lagoons, marshes and estuaries. Its favorite foods are fish and frogs.

Lizard *Sceloporus malachiticus*
[OPPOSITE, LEFT]
CHIAPAS, MEXICO • Small, harmless lizards are among the most common reptiles seen in the rainforest.

Mantis family *Mantidae*
[OPPOSITE, RIGHT]
LAGUNAS DE MONTEBELLO NATIONAL PARK, CHIAPAS, MEXICO • Small carnivores which hunt in the forest understory.

Leaf-cutter Ants *genus Atta*
[TOP LEFT]
These minute beasts are able to defoliate an entire tree in a few days.

Giant Centipede family *Scolopendra*
[TOP RIGHT]
MAYA MOUNTAINS FOREST RESERVE, BELIZE • These aggressive carnivores are equipped with two poison-exuding fangs used to subdue prey.

Tiger Gecko family *Gekkonidae*
[CENTER LEFT]
COSMOS CAMPGROUND, CAYO DISTRICT, BELIZE • These small lizards are equipped with suction-like scales on their feet allowing them to defy gravity.

Tiger Tarantula family *Theraphosidae*
[CENTER RIGHT]
DEININGER NATIONAL PARK, EL SALVADOR • Nocturnal predators with a mildly poisonous bite.

Tropical Rattlesnake *Crotalus durissus*
[BOTTOM LEFT]
LAKE ATITLÁN NATIONAL PARK, GUATEMALA • Known as the "royal viper" this is the largest kind of rattlesnake. Highly venomous.

Green Iguanid Lizard *Laemactus longipes*
[BOTTOM RIGHT]
PALENQUE NATIONAL PARK, CHIAPAS, MEXICO • Excellent camouflage gives this medium-sized reptile near invisibilty.

Leaf Beetle
family *Chrysomlidae*
[LEFT]
LAKE ATITLÁN NATIONAL PARK,
GUATEMALA • One of the most
diverse of beetle families in the
tropics with thousands of species.

Passion Fruit Flower
[TOP RIGHT]
MAYA MOUNTAINS FOREST RESERVE,
BELIZE

Terrestrial Orchid
Laelia digbyana
[BOTTOM RIGHT]
TAK-BE-HA NATURE RESERVE,
QUINTANA ROO, MEXICO

Wild Orchid *Lycaste sp.*
[OPPOSITE, TOP LEFT]
ALTA VERAPAZ PROVINCE, GUATEMALA

Miniature Crab Spider
family *Thomicidae*
with Maya Stingless Bee
[OPPOSITE, RIGHT]
COSMOS CAMPRGROUND NATURE
RESERVE, CAYO, BELIZE • This tiny spider assumes the color of the flower
it is on. Perfectly camouflaged, it
lays in wait for nectar
seeking bees.

Wildflower
Tradescantia crassifolia
[OPPOSITE, BOTTOM LEFT]
AZUL MEAMBAR NATIONAL PARK,
HONDURAS

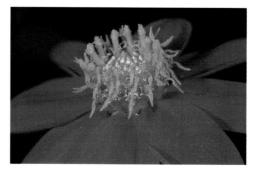

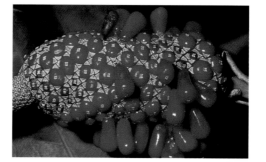

Wildflower
[LEFT]
Maya Mountains, Belize

Wildflower
Mimosa albida
[TOP RIGHT]
Maya Mountains, Belize

Wildflower
Dahlia coccinea
[CENTER RIGHT]
Cuero Y Salado Wildlife
Refuge, Honduras

Wild Fruit
[BOTTOM RIGHT]
Tikal National Park,
Guatemala

Orchid
[OPPOSITE, TOP LEFT]
Alta Verapaz, Guatemala

Hibiscus Flower
Hibiscus rosa-sinensis
[OPPOSITE, RIGHT]
Maya Mountains, Belize

Blue Morpho Butterfly
Morpho peleides
[OPPOSITE, BOTTOM LEFT]
Pico Bonito National Park,
Honduras

Loggerhead Seaturtle *Caretta caretta*
[TOP LEFT]
XCACEL NATURE RESERVE, QUINTANA ROO, MEXICO • Baby turtle makes its way towards the open ocean shortly after hatching.

Manatee *Treichechus manatus*
[BOTTOM LEFT]
HICKS CAY, BELIZE • The largest aquatic herbivore in Central America.

Jellyfish
[BOTTOM RIGHT]
EL CUCO BEACH, EL SALVADOR

Rio Largartos National Park
[OPPOSITE]
YUCATÁN, MEXICO

Agua Azul Nature Reserve
[TOP LEFT]
CHIAPAS, MEXICO • Cold water plunging down from the mountains flows through the steamy jungle at Agua Azul.

Palenque National Park
[BOTTOM LEFT]
CHIAPAS, MEXICO

Bacalar Lagoon
[OPPOSITE]
QUINTANA ROO, MEXICO

Pacaya Volcano National Park, Guatemala
[OPPOSITE, LEFT]
One of the most active volcanoes in Central America, Pacaya often treats visitors to a fiery display.

El Salto Falls
[OPPOSITE, RIGHT]
ALTA VERAPAZ PROVINCE, GUATEMALA

Tok' Be Ha' Cave
[TOP RIGHT]
QUINTANA ROO, MEXICO • Tok' Be Ha' means "hidden waters" in Maya. This cave is part of one of the largest underground systems ever explored. It is located near the ruins of Tulum.

Cenote Xkeken
[BOTTOM RIGHT]
YUCATÁN, MEXICO • Cenotes are created when the roof of a cavern caves in, forming a sink hole. The Itzá-Maya of the Yucatán have always considered them sacred, and this is understandable in a region of arid limestone plains where there are virtually no rivers. These cool, subterranean pools have been their main source of water.

Izalco Volcano
[TOP LEFT]
CERRO VERDE NATIONAL PARK, EL SALVADOR • The sunrise casts a red hue over Izalco. In the distance you can see the Pacific coastline through the mist.

Fuego Volcano National Park
[BOTTOM LEFT]
GUATEMALA • One of Guatemala's three active volcanoes, Fuego is usually seen with a plume of vapor and smoke belching from its crater. In the distance can be seen the chain of volcanic cones which line the coast, part of the Pacific Rim circle of fire.

Moonlight Vista over the Polochic Valley
[OPPOSITE]
ALTA VERAPAZ PROVINCE, GUATEMALA • This splendid view was obtained from the crest of the Sierra Yalihúx Mountains at an elevation of nearly nine thousand feet. In the distance, clouds cascade down the slopes of the Piedras Blancas Mountains.

The First People

The origin of the Maya continues to be a mystery. Evidence from recent genetic research has provided strong proof that all humans on Earth share a single root ancestry. The genetic "Adam and Eve," the great, great grandparents of all of us may have lived as recently as 35,000 years ago and certainly not more than 400,000 years ago in Africa or Asia. The record of early human migration patterns is far from being clear. What we do know is that during the last Ice Age—which lasted approximately 90,000 years and ended around 12,000 years ago—so much water was locked up in the great glaciers that the world's oceans were much lower than we find them today thus exposing above the waves dry land totaling an area larger than the size of contemporary Africa. Asia was joined with North America by the Bering land bridge. Most scholars believe that the first Mesoamericans arrived as the result of Neolithic migrations—on foot—out of Asia, through North America and finally, after thousands of years, reaching Central America. These migrations began before the end of the Ice Age and possibly as long as 50,000 years ago. As the glaciers melted a tremendous surge of icy water flooded the oceans and the Caribean Sea rose by at least 130 feet. Great islands as well as enormous sections of the mainland were rapidly inundated. Some researchers see here the possible origin of the story of the flood in the Bible as well as the supposedly mythical accounts of islands such as Atlantis and Lemuria. Is it possible that the first Mesoamericans arrived not by foot but by sea? One day these questions will be resolved by competent archeologists.

Remains of Mastodon at the Huehuetenango site
[RIGHT]

Neolithic period hand prints at Loltún Cavern
[OPPOSITE]

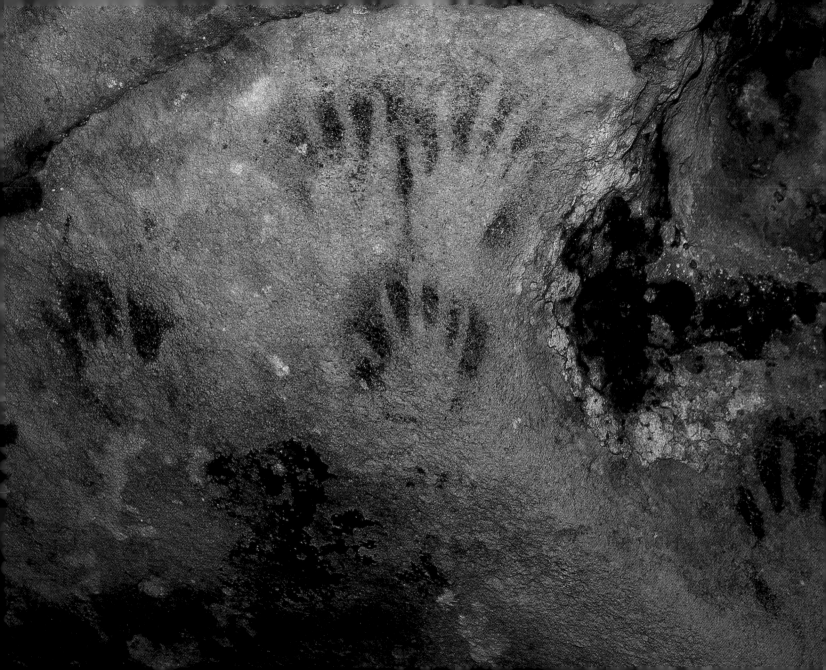

For now all we have are hypotheses. It is interesting to note that the earliest known settlement in the Americas is found at the Valdivia site in Equador. First inhabited at least 12,500 years ago, most scientists concur that humans were present at Valdivia by 20,000 B.C.

Concrete evidence of the first Mesoamerican people comes from several archeological finds: Octavio Alvarado Villatoro was digging a well and encountered some weird bones on his property located near the Guatemalan town of Huehuetenango. He decide to call the university and eventually a team of Canadian researchers excavated the site. They were astonished by what they discovered: the remains of several mastodon associated with primitive stone tools dating to approximately 10,000 B.C. More recently, Mexican scientists excavating the floor of Loltún Cavern in the State of Yucatán encountered the hoof of a small Pleistocene horse and part of a mastodon tusk and molar along with crudely fashioned Neolithic tools made of wood and bone also dating from around 10,000 B.C. These first colonists left silent testimony of their presence on the cave walls in the form of hand prints.

By 5,000 B.C. the early settlers had achieved the domestication of a variety of edible plants including maize, beans, squash, tomatoes, chilies, and avocados. But not until 2,000 B.C. do we find evidence of a fully developed agricultural economy and permanently settled villages. Among the earliest known settlements are those of Cuello in Northern Belize and San Lorenzo on the Gulf coast of Tabasco State. Both were well established by 1500 B.C. Then, rather suddenly around 1,300 B.C., the Olmec culture appears with a level of sociopolitical complexity previously unknown in the region. Monumental architecture, rich tombs, jade figurines, and the enigmatic colossal heads all give testimony of the vibrant Olmec culture which flourished then. Olmec influence extended far beyond the sites of San Lorenzo and La Venta and can be seen in artifacts found along the Pacific coasts of Chiapas and Guatemala where the Ocos culture thrived. By 600 B.C. the population in the Maya lowlands was growing rapidly and it was during this period when the sites of the great Maya cities such as Tikal, Calakmul, and Uaxactun were first settled. But not until the "Chuen Period," between 200 and 50 B.C. do we see the first construction of large ceremonial buildings. By around 100 B.C. the first temple structures at the North Acropolis of Tikal had been built and the Great Plaza was as large and formal as in Late Classic times. Magnificent cities emerged from the jungle and society became stratified into distinct classes: priests, nobles, peasant farmers, artisans, and slaves. Art and science flourished and the achievements of the Maya rivaled

Prehistoric Ceramic Figurine
[BELOW]
CHIAPAS, MEXICO • An ancient culture flourished along the Pacific coasts of Chiapas and Guatemala and pre-dated the Olmec. This figurine is thought to have been a shamans fetish.

Prehistoric Ceramic Figurine
[OPPOSITE, TOP LEFT]
CHIAPAS, MEXICO • This enigmatic face was created by the pre-Olmec Mokaya culture and exhibits physical characteristics which do not look Mayan.

La Venta
[OPPOSITE, BOTTOM LEFT]
TABASCO, MEXICO • Seated figure with stylized rattlesnake.

Colossal Head from La Venta
(circa 900 B.C.)
[OPPOSITE, FAR RIGHT]
TABASCO, MEXICO • These enormous "baby face" carvings were a common theme of Olmec artisans.

any of those of the old world. In fact, many similarities can be seen between classic Maya culture and its counterparts in Egypt, Mesopotamia, India and China.

By the year 800 A.D., for reasons at present poorly understood Maya civilization began to decline. Ecological degradation causing crops to fail, inter-city warring, peasant revolt, plagues and earthquakes are among the theories put forward by scholars in explanation. The ceremonial centers were successively abandoned, starting in the South and moving progressively northward to the area know today as Puc. In 925, at the same time when all the great Classic cities were being reclaimed by the jungle, a cultural resurgence was beginning in the North of the Yucatán Peninsula and new and even more sophisticated cities began to appear. During this period Toltecs from their capital of

The Winged Disc
This symbol originated in ancient Egypt and often appeared in the artistic works of the classic Vedic culture of India. Note the striking similarity between the Egyptian version (above) and those from the Maya ruins of Tikal (middle) and a site near Ocosingo, Chiapas (below).

Tula arrived in the Yucatán and their influence can be seen in the monumental art of several Maya centers, especially at Chichén Itzá. In 1002 a federation of Maya city-states was formed which included Chichén, Mayapan, Uxmal, and Izmal. The federation brought a period of peace and prosperity to the Maya of Yucatán. The alliance ended when war erupted between Chichén Itzá and Mayapan with the latter claiming victory around the year 1190. At this time the centers of Uxmal, Kabah, Chichén and Izmal were abandoned and soon green luxuriance overtook them. Mayapan continued as the focal point of cultural influence until 1441 when almost all the peninsular inhabitants rose in rebellion. Mayapan was defeated and plundered and the peninsula became divided into 19 chiefdoms. Then, in 1540, the Spanish "Conquistadors" arrived and, in the name of god, the Holy Roman Catholic Church and the King of Spain they proceeded to conquer and subjugate as best they could. On June 16, 1562 the Bishop of Yucatán, Diego de Landa, issued an *Auto-da-Fe* declaring all Maya religious artifacts as well as all their books to be "of the devil," and in a ceremony carried out in front of the church at Maní they were burned. Thus the opportunity to learn more about the ancient Maya culture was lost forever. During this traumatic period the indigenous population was ravaged by European brought diseases such as small pox and influenza for which they had little resistance. It is estimated that more than 90% of the native population perished during the first hundred years of occupation. Still, according to the way the Maya view things, they were never "conquered." The Maya have always resisted the foreign occupation of their territories and that resistance continues today. Incredibly, almost miraculously, Maya culture continues as a vibrant reality: the attestation of the tenacity, perseverance, and strength of the Maya people.

La Venta
(circa 900 B.C.)
[TOP LEFT]
TABASCO, MEXICO • Cache of jade figurines found buried at La Venta site on the Gulf coast. Thought to be a sacrificial offering.

La Venta
(circa 900 B.C.)
[TOP RIGHT]
TABASCO, MEXICO • Basalt "altar."

Abaj Takalik
(circa 600 B.C.)
[BOTTOM RIGHT]
RETALHULEU PROVINCE, GUATEMALA • Olmec-style colossal heads sometimes weighed as much as 20 tons. Many archeologists believe that these strange faces actually represented "were-jaguars", the melding of a human with his animal nagual.

Abaj Takalik
(circa 600 B.C.)
[BOTTOM LEFT]
RETALHULEU PROVINCE, GUATEMALA • Large zoomorph, probably a toad or frog.

La Venta (circa 900 B.C.)
[TOP LEFT]
TABASCO, MEXICO

La Venta (circa 900 B.C.)
[TOP CENTER]
TABASCO, MEXICO

El Baul (circa 200 B.C.)
[TOP RIGHT]
PACIFIC COAST, GUATEMALA

San Raymundo
(circa 200 B.C.)
[BOTTOM RIGHT]
PACIFIC COAST, GUATEMALA

La Democracia
(circa 200 B.C.)
[BOTTOM CENTER]
PACIFIC COAST, GUATEMALA

El Baul(circa 200 B.C.)[
BOTTOM LEFT]
PACIFIC COAST, GUATEMALA

Cuello
[TOP RIGHT]
ORANGE WALK DISTRICT, BELIZE • The site of a village first established as early as 2500 B.C. Pottery found here is the earliest known from Mesoamerica.

La Venta (circa 900 B.C.)
[BOTTOM RIGHT]
TABASCO, MEXICO

Cahal Pech
[BOTTOM CENTER]
CAYO DISTRICT, BELIZE • Obsidian tools and offerings. Maya craftsmen developed obsidian knives as sharp as a razor.

La Venta (circa 900 B.C.)
[BELOW LEFT]
TABASCO, MEXICO • Enigmatic "mustached" figure carved in basalt.

Tikal National Park
[TOP LEFT]
GUATEMALA • Unrestored pre-Classic temple.

Tikal National Park
[BELOW]
GUATEMALA • Giant pre-Classic masks buried below the North Acropolis.

Tikal National Park
[BOTTOM LEFT]
GUATEMALA • The pyramid of the Masks located at the western edge of the Great Plaza. Erected around the year 700 A.D. by ruler Ha Sawa Chann.

Tikal National Park
[OPPOSITE]
GUATEMALA • Dawn from atop Temple IV.

Tikal National Park
[LEFT]
GUATEMALA • Temple of the Giant Jaguar.

Tikal National Park
[BELOW]
GUATEMALA • Stela erected in 445 A.D. commemorating King K'awil Chann's (Stormy Sky) rule.

Tikal National Park
[OPPOSITE]
GUATEMALA • Temple of Double-headed Serpent. Classic Period.

Copán
[TOP LEFT]
HONDURAS • Classic Period Stela.

Copán
[TOP CENTER]
HONDURAS • Zoomorph

Quiriguá
[TOP RIGHT]
GUATEMALA • Detail of Classic Period Stela.

Copán
[BOTTOM RIGHT]
HONDURAS • The "old man of Copán" once adorned the Temple of the Inscriptions.

Copán
[BOTTOM CENTER]
HONDURAS • Detail of Classic Period Stela.

Copán
[BOTTOM LEFT]
HONDURAS • Skulls were a popular theme in the monumental art of the Classic Period.

Toniná
[TOP LEFT]
CHIAPAS, MEXICO • Detail of a large stucco panel depicting a macabre scene of human sacrifice and underworld personalities. Classic Period.

Copán
[TOP RIGHT]
HONDURAS • The Storm God. The strange monkey-man holds a torch or scepter featuring the day sign Ik, "wind". Classic Period.

Copán
[BOTTOM RIGHT]
HONDURAS • Skull which adorned a Classic Period Temple.

Toniná
[BOTTOM LEFT]
CHIAPAS, MEXICO • Detail of stucco panel. Classic Period.

Palenque National Park
[TOP LEFT]
CHIAPAS, MEXICO • Temple of the Inscriptions. This pyramid is a monument to the dynasty of Pacal, Palenque's great seventh century ruler. Pacal's crypt lies deep within the structure.

Quiriguá
[BELOW]
GUATEMALA • Detail of Classic Period Stela.

Copán
[BOTTOM LEFT]
HONDURAS • The corbeled vaulted arch was a distinctive feature of Classic Period architecture.

Palenque National Park
[TOP LEFT]
CHIAPAS, MEXICO • Ceramic Mask. Classic
Period.

Palenque National Park
[TOP RIGHT]
CHIAPAS, MEXICO • Ceramic Figure. Classic
Period.

Palenque National Park
[BOTTOM RIGHT]
CHIAPAS, MEXICO • Detail of a large ceramic
censer. Classic Period.

Palenque National Park
[BOTTOM LEFT]
CHIAPAS, MEXICO • Ceramic Figure. Classic
Period.

Palenque National Park
[TOP LEFT]

CHIAPAS, MEXICO • The Palace is thought to have been the administrative center and residential complex of the city-state during its period of glory during the Late Classic Period.

Palenque National Park
[BELOW]

CHIAPAS, MEXICO • Detail of monumental sculpture. The man's arms are crossed across his chest indicating that he is captive or slave. Late Classic Period

Palenque National Park
[BOTTOM LEFT]

CHIAPAS, MEXICO • Temple of the Sun. Late Classis Period.

Ceibal National Park
[BELOW]
EL PETEN PROVINCE, GUATEMALA •
Ornate Classic Period Stela.

Palenque National Park
[RIGHT]
CHIAPAS, MEXICO • An island of pristine rain forest surrounds the ruins.

Kohunlich Ruins
[LEFT]
QUNINTANA ROO, MEXICO

Palenque National Park
[TOP RIGHT]
CHIAPAS, MEXICO • Detail of monumental stone carving.

Uxmal
[BOTTOM RIGHT]
YUCATÁN, MEXICO

Xunantunich
[OPPOSITE, TOP LEFT]
CAYO DISTRICT, BELIZE

Cahal Pech
[OPPOSITE, TOP RIGHT]
CAYO DISTRICT, BELIZE • Classic Period jade mask.

Uxmal
[OPPOSITE, BOTTOM RIGHT]
YUCATÁN, MEXICO • Detail of freize adorning the Nunnery Quadrangle.

Chichén Itzá
[OPPOSITE, BOTTOM CENTER]
YUCATÁN, MEXICO • The enigmatic Chac Mool figure at the entrance of the Temple of the Warriors is thought to have been a sacrificial altar.

Lamanai
[OPPOSITE, BOTTOM LEFT]
ORANGE WALK DISTRICT, BELIZE • Classic Period ceramic bowl.

Uxmal

[OPPOSITE, TOP LEFT]

YUCATÁN, MEXICO • The Palace of the Governor. The statue in the fore-
ground represents two jaguar joined at the breast, pointing north and south.

Chichén Itzá

[OPPOSITE, TOP RIGHT]

YUCATÁN, MEXICO • The Jaguar Throne, Temple of Kukulkan. Painted red
and encrusted with jade, this artifact is located in a secret chamber, appar-
ently an altar room, deep within the pyramid.

Chichén Itzá

[OPPOSITE, BOTTOM RIGHT]

YUCATÁN, MEXICO • The heads of the featherd serpents on either side of
this small temple represent the god Kukulkan, the herald of light and life.

Uxmal

[OPPOSITE, BOTTOM LEFT]

YUCATÁN, MEXICO • Pyramid of the Magician.

Chichén Itzá

[TOP]

YUCATÁN, MEXICO • The Ball Court Complex.

Chichén Itzá

[BOTTOM]

YUCATÁN, MEXICO • Temple of Kukulkan.

Labná
[TOP LEFT]
YUCATÁN, MEXICO • Maya architecture reached new heights of sophistication during the Post Classic renaissance in the region called Puc.

Labná
[BOTTOM RIGHT]
YUCATÁN, MEXICO

Labná
[BOTTOM LEFT]
YUCATÁN, MEXICO

Kabáh
[OPPOSITE]
YUCATÁN, MEXICO • The Codz-Pop Palace. Measuring 45 meters long and 25 meters wide, this structure was certainly one of the most beautiful and highly ornate creations of Post Classic Maya Architects.

Kabáh
[LEFT]
YUCATÁN, MEXICO • Detail of freize adorning the Codz-Pop Palace

Labná
[BOTTOM RIGHT]
YUCATÁN, MEXICO • Detail of Palace freize.

Labná
[BOTTOM LEFT]
YUCATÁN, MEXICO • "Puffy-cheeked" stone figures of the Post Classic era curiously reminiscent of the Olmec style occurring 2500 years earlier.

Mayapan
[OPPOSITE, TOP LEFT]
YUCATÁN, MEXICO • Giant Mask.

Tulum
[OPPOSITE, TOP RIGHT]
QUINTANA ROO, MEXICO • Temple of the Frescos.

Tulum
[OPPOSITE, BOTTOM RIGHT]
QUINTANA ROO, MEXICO • El Castillo.

Sayil
[OPPOSITE, BOTTOM LEFT]
YUCATÁN, MEXICO • The Palace.

Iximché

[TOP LEFT]

TECPÁN PROVINCE, GUATEMALA • A thriving metropolis and capital of the Cak'chiquel Nation when Alvarado arrived in 1524. Angered by finding little gold, he had the Maya chiefs executed and Iximché plundered. On this site the Spanish set up their first capital in Guatemala.

Tulum

[BOTTOM RIGHT]

QUINTANA ROO, MEXICO

Mayapan

[BOTTOM LEFT]

YUCATÁN, MEXICO

Tulum

[OPPOSITE]

QUINTANA ROO, MEXICO

The World of The Maya

The day begins long before dawn in the Maya village. The women stoke the fire which is the heart of their little cottage. There is no chimney or fireplace. The hearth sits in the middle of the hard dirt floor and the smoke wafts up into the rafters and escapes through the soot-blackened roof. The corn, which has been soaking all night in lime water, is stone ground providing the "masa" used to make tortillas and atol: a hot, sweet and thick corn beverage. Conversations take place in hushed tones because the little children like to sleep in. At sunrise the village comes alive. The sounds are those of roosters crowing, dogs barking, children laughing, and always the pat, pat, pat of women making tortillas. The family gathers around the little hearth for a simple breakfast before the men and older boys hike up to the fields to tend to their corn and other crops. The womenfolk remain close to home tending the babies, preparing foods and weaving. By the age of six or seven little girls are already actively participating in the family economy and instead of playing with dolls and making mud pies they are just as often playing with real babies and making real food, which is even more fun. The children are allowed to be part of things which gives them a deep feeling of self-worth and place. Most every day there is time to do some weaving, an age old art passed down from mother to daughter for millenia. For Maya women weaving is full of mystical significance just as for the Maya men the cultivation of corn is much more that simply the production of food. There is no line drawn between the sacred and the mundane. Daily activities proceed ceremonially. By dark the men are back and the family may join together at the little sanctuary which is located at the foot of an ancient tree. There they burn candles and copal incense and commune with the Great Spirit. The high point of the week is market day when the whole family gets dressed up and walks to the regional center. Market day is a time to buy and sell but just as important it is a time to socialize with friends from other villages, swap stories and even meet a potential mate.

San Andrés Xecul

[OPPOSITE]

TOTONICAPAN PROVINCE, GUATEMALA • Maya esthetic sense and symbology meet and blend with Catholic traditions in the Church at Xecul.

Cuchumatanes Mountains
[LEFT]
HUEHUETENANGO PROVINCE, GUATEMALA • Route 9-A, one of the highest roads in Central America, weaves its way between the Cinabal Plateau and Soloma.

Cuchumatanes Mountains
[BOTTOM]
HUEHUETENANGO PROVINCE, GUATEMALA • The village of San Juan Ixcoy is situated in an important apple growing center. Here cool springtime weather predominates year round.

Sololá
[OPPOSITE, TOP LEFT]
SOLOLA PROVINCE, GUATEMALA • The Provincial capital sits perched above the sublime emerald waters of Lake Atitlán. The perfect cone of Atitlán Volcano towers in the distance.

The Chicken Bus
[OPPOSITE, RIGHT]
CHUCHUMATANES MOUNTAINS, GUATEMALA • Affectionately dubbed "chicken bus" because this most used mode of transport often does carry avian passengers. It's a long, bumpy ride from Huehuetenango to the end of the road at Barillas.

Santiago Atitlán
[OPPOSITE, BOTTOM LEFT]
SOLOLÁ PROVINCE, GUATEMALA • Tzutúhil boys race "cayucos" in front of town.

Mam Indian Dwelling
[OPPOSITE, TOP LEFT]
CHUY VILLAGE,
HUEHUETEHANGO
PROVINCE, GUATEMALA

Village of Chiul
[OPPOSITE, TOP RIGHT]
EL QUICHE PROVINCE,
GUATEMALA

Ich-Ek Village
[OPPOSITE, BOTTOM
RIGHT]
YUCATÁN, MEXICO

Ich-Ek Village
[OPPOSITE, BOTTOM
LEFT]
YUCATÁN, MEXICO

Zinacantan
[RIGHT]
CHIAPAS, MEXICO

Road to Puerto Ocós
[BOTTOM LEFT]
SAN MARCOS PROVINCE,
GUATEMALA

Santa Cruz la Laguna
[TOP LEFT]
SOLOLÁ PROVINCE, GUATEMALA • Cak'chiquel women prepare "atol" which is a rich, hot corn beverage.

Chelemhá
[BELOW]
ALTA VERAPAZ PROVINCE, GUATEMALA • Kek'chi woman making a "comal," the griddle she uses to cook tortillas.

Panajachel
[BOTTOM LEFT]
SOLOLÁ PROVINCE, GUATEMALA • Cak'chiquel men, members of the Army reserve, go through weekend exercises.

Chelemhá
[OPPOSITE, LEFT]
ALTA VERAPAZ PROVINCE, GUATEMALA • Kek'chi boy makes a turkey house.

San Juan Chamula
[OPPOSITE, RIGHT]
CHIAPAS, MEXICO • Little shepherd girl.

Naha, Lacandón Jungle
[OPPOSITE, LEFT]
CHIAPAS, MEXICO

Lacantún River
[OPPOSITE, TOP RIGHT]
CHIAPAS, MEXICO • Little Lacandón boy.

Lacanjá, Lacandón Jungle
[OPPOSITE, BOTTOM RIGHT]
CHIAPAS MEXICO • Making tortillas for dinner.

Lacanhá, Lacandón Jungle
[RIGHT]
CHIAPAS MEXICO • Lacandón boy.

Lacanjá, Lacandón Jungle
[BELOW]
CHIAPAS MEXICO • A few years ago the little villages of Lacandonia were very isolated. Now the airwaves have come alive with new community radio stations.

Chichicastenango
[LEFT]
EL QUICHÉ PROVINCE, GUATEMALA • Mayan wedding at an evangelical church.

San Juan Atitán
[BELOW]
HUEHUETENANGO PROVINCE, GUATEMALA • Travelling salesman sells coyote oil pomade, guaranteed to cure all ills.

Chichicastenango
[OPPOSITE, LEFT]
EL QUICHÉ PROVINCE, GUATEMALA • The heart and soul of Guatemalan traditional music: the marimba.

Panajachel
[OPPOSITE, RIGHT]
SOLOLÁ PROVINCE, GUATEMALA • Weekend concert on the shore of Lake Atitlán.

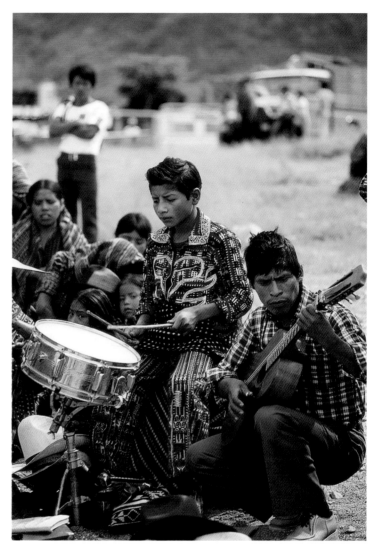

Santiago Sacatepéquez
[TOP]
SACATEPÉQUEZ PROVINCE, GUATEMALA • Cak'chiquel family adorns the grave of a recently deceased relative.

Almolonga
[BOTTOM]
Quetzaltenango Province, Guatemala • Funeral procession.

Zuníl
[OPPOSITE, TOP LEFT]
QUETZALTENANGO PROVINCE, GUATEMALA • Little banana vendor.

Olintepeque
[OPPOSITE, RIGHT]
QUETZALTENANGO PROVINCE, GUATEMALA • Market day.

San Pedro Necta
[OPPOSITE, BOTTOM LEFT]
HUEHUETENANGO PROVINCE, GUATEMALA • Market day.

Esquipulas
[TOP LEFT]
CHIQUIMULA PROVINCE, GUATEMALA • Pilgrims come from all over Guatemala and surrounding countries to venerate the figure of the Black Christ found in the Basilica.

The Black Christ
[BOTTOM RIGHT]

Basilica at Esquipulas
[BOTTOM LEFT]

San Juan Chamula
[OPPOSITE]
CHIAPAS, MEXICO • As in ancient times the temple dominates the settlement's main plaza. The "Catholic" church of Chamula severed all ties with Rome in order to have complete control over their religious practice. Some years ago evangelical missionaries tried to establish themselves in town resulting in a violent conflict. Finally all the evangelicals and their followers were thrown out.

Tikal National Park
[LEFT]
EL PETEN PROVINCE, GUATEMALA • Kek'chi Indians from a nearby village perform sacred rituals in order to insure a successful crop.

Purulhá
[BELOW]
BAJA VERAPAZ, GUATEMALA

San Andrés Xecul
[OPPOSITE, LEFT]
TOTONICAPAN PROVINCE, GUATEMALA • Two jaguars stand above the saint at this Maya Church.

Pascual Abaj, Chichicastenengo
[OPPOSITE, TOP RIGHT]
EL QUICHÉ PROVINCE, GUATEMALA • Ancient place of power.

San Raymundo
[OPPOSITE, BOTTOM RIGHT]
ESCUINTLA PROVINCE, GUATEMALA • This ancient colossal head, dating from 200 B.C. attracts shaman from all over.

Rey San Pascual
[OPPOSITE, LEFT]

GUATEMALA • This figure is often present at Maya shrines. His significance is shrouded in mystery.

Maximón of San Andrés Itzapa
[OPPOSITE, RIGHT]

CHIMALTENANGO PROVINCE, GUATEMALA • It would be hard to find a village or town in highland Guatemala where the presence of Maximon is not felt. But who exactly is Maximon? He is the patron saint of sorcerers. He is Saint Simon. He is Judas Iscariot. He is venerated by hundreds of thousands of Maya. He is barely tolerated by Catholic authorities. Maximon is a true enigma. Many miracles are attributed to him. And his faithful followers rely on him for protection, especially against shaman who cast evil spells.

Maximón of Aguas Calientes
[TOP]

SACATEPÉQUEZ PROVINCE, GUATEMALA

Maximón of Zuníl
[BOTTOM]

QUETZALTENANGO PROVINCE, GUATEMALA

Maximón of Aguas Amargas
[BELOW]

QUETZALTENANGO PROVINCE, GUATEMALA

Threads of Tradition

Weaving and textile production have been an integral part of the Maya culture for thousands of years. The colors and patterns we see today are very different from what would have been seen before contact with the European colonists. Still, many of the symbols used come from the ancient past maintaining a certain continuity through time. The traditional back-srap loom was used to weave thread spun from native "ixcaco" cotton and "ictle" from the agave plant. The Spanish introduced wool and new techniques such as knitting, crocheting, and the vertical foot-loom, all in widespread use today. Each Maya village has its own distinct costume reflecting both old and new in design and color. Ancient stylized figures of plants, animals and supernatural beings appear alongside the weavers rendition of an airplane, helicopter or other artifact of modern culture in today's hybrid motifs. Maya women love bright colors and in recent years flourescent colors, especially hot pink and lime green have appeared on the scene. Most thread used today is industrially produced and dyed. Nevertheless, a resurgence of interest in the use of home-spun cotton and naturally dyed thread is gaining momentum and many women are experimenting with old and nearly forgotten techniques. The male costume is comprised of a hand-woven shirt, belt and pants and sometimes includes a woolen over-skirt worn for added warmth. The womens attire consists of a "huipíl" (blouse), a "corte" (skirt), a "cinta" (belt), and a "tzute" which is a rectangular piece of cloth worn folded on the head or across the shoulder.

Santa Cruz La Laguna, Lake Atitlán
[OPPOSITE]
Sololá Province, Guatemala

San Marcos La Laguna, Lake Atitlán
[LEFT]
SOLOLÁ PROVINCE, GUATEMALA

Todos Santos Cuchumatán
[TOP RIGHT]
HUEHUETENANGO PROVINCE,
GUATEMALA • Weaving the intricate
patterns of a man's shirt lapels
takes place on a back-strap loom.

Todos Santos Cuchumatán
[BOTTOM RIGHT]
HUEHUETENANGO PROVINCE,
GUATEMALA

Ocosingo
[OPPOSITE, TOP LEFT]
CHIAPAS, MEXICO • The foot loom
was introduced by the Spanish and
is in widespread use today.

Xepol
[OPPOSITE, RIGHT]
EL QUICHÉ PROVINCE, GUATEMALA

San Jorge La Laguna
[OPPOSITE, BOTTOM LEFT]
SOLOLÁ PROVINCE, GUATEMALA •
Ixcaco thread being prepared for
weaving.

Todos Santos Cuchumatán
[OPPOSITE, FAR LEFT]
HUEHUETENANGO PROVINCE, GUATEMALA

Santiago Atitlán
[OPPOSITE, TOP]
SOLOLÁ PROVINCE, GUATEMALA

Tenejapa
[OPPOSITE, BOTTOM]
CHIAPAS, MEXICO • Intricate patterns are painstakingly woven into fabric on the back-strap loom.

San Juan Atitán
[TOP LEFT]
HUEHUETENANGO PROVINCE, GUATEMALA

Nahualá
[TOP CENTER]
SOLOLÁ PROVINCE, GUATEMALA

Santa Maria de Jesus
[TOP RIGHT]
SACATEPÉQUEZ PROVINCE, GUATEMALA

Jucanyá
[BOTTOM]
SOLOLÁ PROVINCE, GUATEMALA • Grandmother spins thread from native "ixcaco" cotton.

San Juan Atitán
[LEFT]
HUEHUETENANGO PROVINCE, GUATEMALA

Zinacantán
[TOP RIGHT]
CHIAPAS, MEXICO

Patchitulúl, Lake Atitlán
[BOTTOM RIGHT]
SOLOLÁ PROVINCE, GUATEMALA • Sizing of cotton thread by dunking in a corn-water solution before weaving begins.

Concepción Chiquirichapa
[OPPOSITE]
QUETZALTENANGO PROVINCE, GUATEMALA

San Ildefonso Ixtahuacán
[OPPOSITE, TOP LEFT]
HUEHUETENANGO PROVINCE, GUATEMALA

San Antonio Palopó, Lake Atitlán
[OPPOSITE, TOP CENTER]
SOLOLÁ PROVINCE, GUATEMALA

Chichicastenango
[OPPOSITE, TOP RIGHT]
EL QUICHÉ PROVINCE, GUATEMALA

Sololá
[OPPOSITE, BOTTOM RIGHT]
SOLOLÁ PROVINCE, GUATEMALA

Quetzaltenango (Xelahú)
[OPPOSITE, BOTTOM LEFT]
QUETZALTENANGO PROVINCE, GUATEMALA

San Juan Chamula
[RIGHT]
CHIAPAS, MEXICO

Todos Santos Cuchumatán
[LEFT]
HUEHUETENANGO PROVINCE, GUATEMALA

San Juan Chamula
[BELOW]
CHIAPAS, MEXICO

Palestina de los Altos
[OPPOSITE, LEFT]
QUETZALTENANGO PROVINCE, GUATEMALA

San Rafael Petzel
[OPPOSITE, RIGHT]
HUEHUETENANGO PROVINCE, GUATEMALA

Cobán
[TOP LEFT]
Alta Verapaz Province, Guatemala

Tactíc
[TOP RIGHT]
Alta Verapaz Province, Guatemala

Santa Catarina Palopó
[BOTTOM]
Sololá Province, Guatemala

San Ildefonso Ixtahuacán
[OPPOSITE, LEFT]
Huehuetenango Province, Guatemala

Zuníl
[OPPOSITE, RIGHT]
Quetzaltenango Province, Guatemala

Chichicastenango
[TOP]
EL QUICHÉ PROVINCE, GUATEMALA

Tzununá, Lake Atitlán
[BOTTOM]
SOLOLÁ PROVINCE, GUATEMALA

Camanibal
[OPPOSITE, LEFT]
EL QUICHÉ PROVINCE, GUATEMALA

San Martín Chile Verde
[OPPOSITE, RIGHT]
QUETZALTENANGO PROVINCE, GUATEMALA

San Martín Chile Verde
[LEFT]
QUETZALTENANGO PROVINCE, GUATEMALA

Todos Santos Cuchumatán
[BELOW]
HUEHUETENANGO PROVINCE, GUATEMALA

Almolonga
[OPPOSITE, LEFT]
QUETZALTENANGO PROVINCE, GUATEMALA

San Pedro La Laguna, Lake Atitlán
[OPPOSITE, RIGHT]
SOLOLÁ PROVINCE, GUATEMALA

Concepción Chiquirichapa
[TOP]
QUETZALTENANGO PROVINCE, GUATEMALA

Cancúc
[BOTTOM]
CHIAPAS, MEXICO

Tecpán
[OPPOSITE, LEFT]
CHIMALTENANGO PROVINCE, GUATEMALA

Aguacatán
[OPPOSITE, RIGHT]
HUEHUETENANGO PROVINCE, GUATEMALA

Totonicapán
[OPPOSITE, LEFT]
TOTONICAPÁN PROVINCE, GUATEMALA

Tactíc
[OPPOSITE, RIGHT]
ALTA VERAPÁZ, GUATEMALA

Santiago Sacatepéquez
[TOP]
SACATEPÉQUEZ PROVINCE, GUATEMALA

Tenejapa
[BOTTOM]
CHIAPAS, MEXICO

Almolonga
[LEFT]
QUETZALTENANGO PROVINCE, GUATEMALA

San Jorge La Laguna
[BELOW]
SOLOLÁ PROVINCE, GUATEMALA

La Esperanza
[OPPOSITE, LEFT]
QUETZALTENANGO PROVINCE, GUATEMALA

San Juan La Laguna
[OPPOSITE, RIGHT]
SOLOLÁ PROVINCE, GUATEMALA

Recent Waves of
Colonization

Many scholars are convinced that long-distance ocean voyagers had visited both coasts of Central America by the beginning of the Christian era. And although these Phoenesian, Viking, Chinese, or Polynesian navigators may have in some way contributed to Maya Civilization it was not until the 16th Century that a major new wave of colonization occured with the arrival of the Spanish. Contact between American and European cultures was traumatic to say the least but the eventual amalgamation of the two worlds created a new people: the Mestizo. Later, British colonists arrived. Then settlers from other parts of Europe, Africa, and even Asia made their way to the "New World." The outcome of this mixing and blending of peoples from around the world can be seen in the vibrant and diverse cultural fabric of modern Mesoamerica.

Antigua

[OPPOSITE]

SACATEPÉQUEZ PROVINCE, GUATEMALA • Ruins of the Hermitage of Santa Rosa de Lima.

Antigua
[TOP LEFT]
SACATEPÉQUEZ PROVINCE, GUATEMALA • Detail of a baroque style altar. Church of San Francisco.

Antigua
[TOP RIGHT]
SACATEPÉQUEZ PROVINCE, GUATEMALA • Detail of a baroque style altar. Church of San Francisco.

Antigua
[BOTTOM RIGHT]
SACATEPÉQUEZ PROVINCE, GUATEMALA • Colonial period stucco on wood.

Antigua
[BOTTOM LEFT]
SACATEPÉQUEZ PROVINCE, GUATEMALA • The Virgin of Guadalupe. Church of San Francisco.

Quetzaltenango (Xelahu)
[OPPOSITE, TOP LEFT]
QUETZALTENANGO PROVINCE, GUATEMALA • The Cathedral.

Chetumal
[OPPOSITE, RIGHT]
QUINTANA ROO, MEXICO • This statue stands at the entrance to the city and is entitled "Chetumal: cradle of Mestizaje." According to history it was here where the first Spanish man took an Indian wife thus beginning a new "mestizo" race.

Antigua
[OPPOSITE, BOTTOM LEFT]
SACATEPÉQUEZ PROVINCE, GUATEMALA • In its day Antigua was one of the greatest cities in the Spanish colonial empire, rivaling Lima and Mexico in importance. It was the capital of the "Capitanía General de Coathemala", which included all of Central America and Chiapas.

Panajachél
[TOP LEFT]
SOLOLÁ PROVINCE, GUATEMALA • Every December 7th the people burn the devil in the streets. This tradition, which was brought over from Spain, is thought to exorcise evil spirits.

Rio Tatín
[TOP CENTER]
IZABÁL PROVINCE, GUATEMALA • Don Juan claims that his ancestry includes pirates, Indians, and Spanish.

La Libertad
[TOP RIGHT]
EL SALVADOR • Ladino woman sells boiled corn on the beach.

Esquipulas
[BOTTOM RIGHT]
CHIQUIMULA PROVINCE, GUATEMALA • Spanish priest blesses a pick-up with holy water.

Sta. Lucia Cotzumalguapa, Guatemala
[BOTTOM LEFT]
Sugar refinery.

Punta Cocolí
[OPPOSITE]
IZABÁL PROVINCE, GUATEMALA • Little ladino fisherman greets the dawn.

The New Nation of Belize

Belize is so different from its neighbors that it deserves a chapter of its own. British buccaneers (buccan is the Maya word for manatee meat) got a foothold along the Caribbean coast of Central America during the 17th Century and the area soon became a favorite refuge for pirate ships preying on Spanish merchant vessels. Later on, permanent logging camps were established along the coast to satisfy the growing European demand for tropical hardwood. The early colonists became known as the Baymen. Hostilities between British and the Spanish culminated in 1798 when the Governor of Yucatán sent a fleet of 30 warships to rout the settlers and on September 10th a fierce battle took place at St. George Cay, which is located on the reef just east of present day Belize City. Almost miraculously the Baymen were to prevail and send the Spanish running. The victory left the Baymen jubilant and proved to be the crucial event in establishing "British Honduras" as independent from "New Spain." But it was not until May 12, 1862 that the colony was officially founded by the authority of the Queen of England. Both Mexico and Guatemala have disputed the legality of Britian's claim to Belize. In fact, the Guatemalan constitution proclaims that Belize is part of Guatemala. Territorial integrity has been maintained over the years by the strong presence of the British Armed Forces. On September 21, 1981 Belize became an independent country within the British Commonwealth. English speaking, democratic and peaceful, Belize is a land where cultural diversity is seen as a strength and where politics, soccer, and ecology are the national passions.

The Barrier Reef
[OPPOSITE]
Belize is blessed with one of the most extensive reef sytems in the world. Here divers explore a submarine canyon. (Photo courtesy Carol Small.)

El Pilar
[TOP LEFT]
Cayo District • Maya Culture day. Local comedians entertain the crowd.

El Pilar
[TOP CENTER]
Cayo District • Maya Culture Day. The dance of the Hogs' head.

Dangriga
[TOP RIGHT]
Stann Creek District • Three generations of Mopan Maya women perform traditional dances at the District Day Celebration.

Belize Defense Force
[BOTTOM RIGHT]
On parade.

We've won
[BOTTOM LEFT]
The Peoples United Party (PUP) takes over City Hall in San Ignacio, Cayo District.

Toledo District Day
[OPPOSITE, LEFT]
Ancient art of "belly rolling" is demonstrated.

Stann Creek District Day
[OPPOSITE, TOP RIGHT]
Nigerian style dance performed by girls from Gales Point Manatee.

Stann Creek District Day
[OPPOSITE, BOTTOM RIGHT]
Who can make it to the bottle of rum at the end of the greasy pole.?

Welcome to Gales Point
[OPPOSITE, LEFT]
BELIZE DISTRICT • The picturesque village of Gales Point is situated on a penninsula in the middle of Manatee Lagoon.

Gales Point Post Office
[OPPOSITE, TOP RIGHT]

Belize River Ferry
[OPPOSITE, BOTTOM RIGHT]
CAYO DISTRICT • Because Belize has a small population and relatively few vehicles small ferries are the most economical means of crossing the river. This road takes you to the Mennonite settlement of Spanish Lookout.

Ambergris Cay
[TOP]
Local fishing boat cruises in front of San Pedro Town.

Belize City
[BOTTOM]
The heart of Belize City is at the Swing Bridge which spans the Belize River. Every morning and evening the bridge is manually cranked open to let boats pass.

Garífuna Vibrations

Inhabiting the Caribbean coast along Belize, Guatemala, and Honduras, the Garífuna people trace their history back to the island of St. Vincent in the West Indies. In 1635 two Spanish vessels carrying slaves taken from Nigeria were shipwrecked off the island. Some of the slaves managed to swim to shore and survive. These refugees soon inter-married with the island's natives, the descendents of Arawak and Kalipuna (Carib) Indians. Their offspring became known as Black Caribs and though strongly African in appearance they spoke the Arawakan language. These people were fiercely independent and fought many battles against the British colonial authorities. In 1796 the British forces, considering it to be inconvenient to allow a free black society to exist alongside slave-owning European settlers, decided to deport all Black Caribs. They were hunted down, put on ships, and eventually sent to Honduras. One of the ships was captured by the Spanish and taken to the port of Trujillo. The others made it to the island of Roatan where the British had a colony. Over the years the Black Caribs, today preferring to be called Garífuna or Garinagu, have established settlements up and down the coast and have managed to preserve many aspects of their African and Amerindian cultural traditions. In recent years there has been a kind of cultural revival among the Garífuna and traditional music, dance, foods, and dress are all making a comeback. In Belize, the largely Garífuna town of Stann Creek was recently re-named Dangriga, a Garífuna word for "standing waters." Garífuna Settlement Day is the biggest celebration of the year and is held every November 19th.

Miami Village
[OPPOSITE]
ATLANTIDA PROVINCE, HONDURAS • This small Garifuna settlement is much the same as it would have been found 200 years ago when first inhabited.

Toledo District Day
[OPPOSITE, LEFT]
Little Garífuna girl, part of the Ebolite Dance Troop, entertains guests with Afro-caribbean styles.

Dangriga
[OPPOSITE, RIGHT]
STANN CREEK DISTRICT • Garífuna women prepares "Hudut" which is prepared from mashed plantains and usually served with "Bondiga," a rich coconut fish soup.

Dangriga
[TOP]
STANN CREEK DISTRICT • "L.K.", The Lyrical King, the master Rasta rapper from Placencia keeps the crowd jumpin' at the festival.

Stann Creek District Day
[BOTTOM]
Garífuna girls dance group from the village of Barranco.

Trujillo
[OPPOSITE, TOP LEFT]
COLÓN PROVINCE, HONDURAS • The original Garífuna settlement in America.

Dangriga Town
[OPPOSITE, TOP RIGHT]
STANN CREEK DISTRICT, BELIZE • One of the largest centers of Garífuna culture.

Seine Bight Village
[OPPOSITE, BOTTOM RIGHT]
STANN CREEK DISTRICT, BELIZE

Punta Sal
[OPPOSITE, BOTTOM LEFT]
ATLANTIDA PROVINCE, HONDURAS • Garífuna woman returns to Miami village.

Amatique Bay
[TOP]
IZABÁL PROVINCE, GUATEMALA • Garífuna fishermen from Livingston work the bay.

The Mosquito Coast
[BOTTOM]
ATLANTIDA PROVINCE, HONDURAS

Festivals and Celebrations

Without question the biggest celebration of the year occurs during Holy Week when every town and village hosts elaborate processions where images of the saints are paraded through the streets accompanied by musicians playing traditional songs of both Maya and European origin. In many places elaborate carpets, painstakingly constructed of colored sawdust and fragrant flowers, cover the major avenues only to be destroyed by the passing parade. Carnival is also among the important celebrations and becomes a massive party in places like Merida, Cozumel, Mazatenango, and La Ceiba. Each town and village also has their own yearly festival, usually held on the day of their patron saint, when all the residents, dressed up in their finest clothing, converge upon the plaza where games, exotic foods, music and the crowning of the new queen all contribute to making the day special.

Chiapa de Corzo
[RIGHT]
CHIAPAS, MEXICO • Los Parachicos.

Mérida
[OPPOSITE]
YUCATÁN, MEXICO • The streets come alive during February with the massive carnival celebration, one of the biggest in the Americas.

Mérida
[LEFT]
YUCATÁN, MEXICO • Carnival.

Mérida
[OPPOSITE, LEFT]
YUCATÁN, MEXICO • Carnival.

Mérida
[OPPOSITE, RIGHT]
YUCATÁN, MEXICO • Carnival.

Mérida
[OPPOSITE, LEFT]
YUCATÁN, MEXICO • Carnival.

Mazatenango
[OPPOSITE, RIGHT]
SUCHITEPÉQUEZ PROVINCE, GUATEMALA • The Carnival at "Mazate" is
relatively small in size but the spirit of the people make up for any
lack of sophistication. Carnival at Mazate is a blast.

Mazatenango
[RIGHT]
SUCHITEPÉQUEZ PROVINCE, GUATEMALA • Carnival.

Mazatenango
[LEFT]
SUCHITEPÉQUEZ PROVINCE, GUATEMALA • Carnival.

Mazatenango
[OPPOSITE, TOP LEFT]
SUCHITEPÉQUEZ PROVINCE, GUATEMALA • Carnival.

Panajachél
[OPPOSITE, TOP RIGHT]
SOLOLÁ PROVINCE, GUATEMALA • During the celebration of "Corpus Christi" pandemonium reigns in the streets of "Pana." Here Ronald Reagan joins an Indian man in drag during a crazy dance right out of the insane asylum. The exact reason and purpose of these dances defy interpretation.

Panajachél
[OPPOSITE, BOTTOM RIGHT]
SOLOLÁ PROVINCE, GUATEMALA • Corpus Celebration.

Mazatenango
[OPPOSITE, BOTTOM LEFT]
SUCHITEPÉQUEZ PROVINCE, GUATEMALA • Carnival.

Chichicastenango
[TOP LEFT]
EL QUICHÉ PROVINCE, GUATEMALA • Holy Week Procession.

Antigua
[BOTTOM LEFT]
SACATEPÉQUEZ PROVINCE, GUATEMALA • Holy Week Procession.

Antigua
[OPPOSITE, TOP LEFT]
SACATEPÉQUEZ PROVINCE, GUATEMALA • Holy Week Procession.

Antigua
[OPPOSITE, RIGHT]
SACATEPÉQUEZ PROVINCE, GUATEMALA • Holy Week Procession.

Antigua
[OPPOSITE, BOTTOM LEFT]
SACATEPÉQUEZ PROVINCE, GUATEMALA • Holy Week Procession.

Santiago Atitlán
[OPPOSITE, LEFT]
SOLOLÁ PROVINCE, GUATEMALA • Jesus is crucified.

Santiago Atitlán
[OPPOSITE, TOP RIGHT]
SOLOLÁ PROVINCE, GUATEMALA • Holy Week Celebration. Maximon is brought out to meet the Christ.

Santiago Atitlán
[OPPOSITE, BOTTOM RIGHT]
SOLOLÁ PROVINCE, GUATEMALA • Holy Week Procession.

Livingston
[TOP LEFT]
IZABÁL PROVINCE, GUATEMALA • Christ is taken captive.

Livingston
[RIGHT]
IZABÁL PROVINCE, GUATEMALA • Holy Week Procession.

Livingston
[BOTTOM LEFT]
IZABÁL PROVINCE, GUATEMALA • The Roman Centurian.

Baile De La Conquista

Also known as the "Dance of the Moors," the Baile de la Conquista is performed once a year in each Indian village. The dance is always accompanied by the ceaseless drone of the marimba, base drum and an oboe-like instrument called the "chirimía" and it may commence in the morning or afternoon, perhaps continuing all night. It is considered a great privilege for a man or boy to be selected by committee to be one of the dancers. Among the characters represented in the dance are Pedro de Alvarado, the infamous Spanish conquistador who ordered many Indian chiefs crucified and initiated nearly five hundred years of slavery and oppression of the Maya. Tecún Uman, the great Maya chief slain on the battlefield of Xelahu by Alvarado, is accompanied by a shaman as well as by several jaguars, deer and dogs. The dogs are usually played by small boys and are the clowns of the dance. While the performance is not choreogrphed in any discernable way, there are favorite themes that are enacted over and over throughout the day, such as a jaguar carrying away a Spanish woman and two deer sparring.

Tzalamilá
[TOP LEFT]
ALTA VERAPAZ PROVINCE, GUATEMALA

San Juan La Laguna
[BOTTOM LEFT]
SOLOLÁ PROVINCE, GUATEMALA

La Esperanza
[OPPOSITE LEFT]
QUETZALTENANGO PROVINCE, GUATEMALA

La Esperanza
[OPPOSITE RIGHT]
QUETZALTENANGO PROVINCE, GUATEMALA

Chiapa de Corzo

[TOP LEFT]

CHIAPAS, MEXICO • The Parachicos celebration. Traditional woman's costume.

Panajachél

[RIGHT]

SOLOLÁ PROVINCE, GUATEMALA • Dancers dressed up as Martians, crocodiles, political figures, and even Moses take part during the celebration of "Convite" during December.

Todos Santos Cuchumatán

[BOTTOM LEFT]

HUEHUETENANGO PROVINCE, GUATEMALA • Little girl in ceremonial costume. All Saints Day.

Chichicastenango

[OPPOSITE, LEFT]

EL QUICHÉ PROVINCE, GUATEMALA • El Palo Volador, the "flying pole" is an ancient ceremony still preserved in some villages. Here the performace marks the 1997 signing of a peace accord between the government and the guerrillas.

Santiago Sacatepéquez

[OPPOSITE, TOP RIGHT]

SACATEPÉQUEZ PROVINCE, GUATEMALA • Giant kites called "barriletes" are flown on All Saints Day from the cemetary.

Laguna Chicabál

[OPPOSITE, BOTTOM RIGHT]

QUETZALTENANGO PROVINCE, GUATEMALA • Every year exactly forty days after Holy Sunday, shaman or "brujos" from around the highlands meet at this volcanic crater lake to perform sacred ceremonies. Called the Festival of the Holy Cross, this event is thought to have pre-Columbian origins.

Laguna Chicabál

[TOP]

QUETZALTENANGO PROVINCE, GUATEMALA • Festival of the Holy Cross.

Laguna Chicabál

[BOTTOM]

QUETZALTENANGO PROVINCE, GUATEMALA • Festival of the Holy Cross.

Winds of Change:
Mesoamerica Enters the 21st Century

The land of the ancient Maya is a place of unexelled beauty, diversity and magic but in order to provide a balanced view of the region it is necessary to reflect also on some of the deep problems besetting mesoamerica. Among the worst of these include widespread poverty exacerbated by a rapidly growing population, a socioeconomic system which favors a small wealthy elite at the expense of the *campesino* majority, a political system which largely excludes participation by indigenous people, government corruption at all levels, and ecological degradation due to ineffective environmental law enforcement. It is widely acknowledged that peace and stability will not flower in the region until native people are treated fairly and allowed full representation in government. Although there have been some improvements in recent decades, a visit to the halls of congress in any of the countries will quickly reveal that the Maya have very little presence there. Extreme poverty inevitably leads to peasant rebellion and as peace accords are signed new guerrilla groups, manned by young dissidents, are emerging.

We should also mention some of the positive trends becoming visible during recent years. These include ever increasing freedom of speech and expression throughout the region, a growing ecology movement with dozens of conservation groups being established, recent crackdowns on corrupt military and government officials and an atmosphere of cultural revival among the indigenous people of the land. All elements necessary for a prosperous and peaceful future are abundantly present. It is up to each one of us to make sure that the principals of justice, honesty, empathy, and above all, love, prevail on our 8,000 mile diameter blue-green home. Finally, and to invoke the words of the Maya Elders: "We will learn to obey the law of *Tatixel* (Creator-God) or perish."

Guatemala City
[LEFT]
Campesinos protesting working conditions and demanding land reform in front of the National Palace. 1996.

San Cristobal
[OPPOSITE]
CHIAPAS, MEXICO • Childrens Peace March. 1997.

Maya Biosphere Reserve
[TOP LEFT]
GUATEMALA • Campesinos invade the reserve looking for land to farm.

The Mexican Army
[TOP RIGHT]
SAN CRISTOBAL, CHIAPAS, MEXICO

Zapatista Rebels
[BOTTOM RIGHT]
LACANDÓN JUNGLE, CHIAPAS, MEXICO
(Zapatista photos courtesy Perfil Urbano)

Maya Indian Protest
[BOTTOM LEFT]
SOLOLÁ, GUATEMALA

Working for Peace
[OPPOSITE, LEFT]

Olintepeque
[OPPOSITE, TOP RIGHT]
QUETZALTENANGO PROVINCE, GUATEMALA • Youth ecology group cleans up the river area.

Aldea El Xab
[OPPOSITE, BOTTOM RIGHT]
RETALHULEU PROVINCE, GUATEMALA • Campesino invaders take over private estate.